Man, Ships, and the Sea

MAN, SHIPS, *and* THE SEA

A collection of poems by

JOSEPH L. BENSINGER

Second Edition

Copyright © 2022 Joseph L. Bensinger
Second edition

jben775@currently.com

ISBN 978-1-7377045-3-9

Edited and designed by Tell Tell Poetry

Printed in the United States of America

First Printing, 2022

For Twila, Jennifer, and Jesse—
three special rovers of life.

CONTENTS

As Though It Were Written in Sand

ACKNOWLEDGMENTS

To my wife, Twila, who helped to turn my scribbled notes and drafts into a shade of coherence, weaving a tapestry amongst my disparate thoughts—

To my children, Jennifer and Jesse, for their support—

And to Tell Tell Poetry, who made my manuscript intelligible and provided the encouragement to work through the grit of editing—

Thank you!

ACKNOWLEDGEMENTS

DEEP BLUE *and* SUN-BRIGHT

SEA SONG

Give me the wild and rolling breakers
and the foam that laps the sea.
Give me the hues of green and blue
and the clouds flying white and free.

Give me the breath upon my sail
of the wind's fierce sweeping pace.
Give me the surge to fill my soul
and down the combs I'll race.

Give me the whistling born of winds
as the bubbling spray does soar.
Give me the slapping and pounding waves
that rally this musical roar.

Give me the freedom of these sways
and the rhythm that sets the score.
Give me this dancing on the seas
and I'll wish for land no more.

SPINDRIFT

Over the moon, the dark clouds slide.
Alive are the nymphs riding the tide.
Spiritual doings on this side of the strand.
Drowned sailors and mermaids play in the sand.

Sea sprites in the surf dance a frolicsome jig,
reeling and rocking all over the brig,
splashing the wavelets high in the air,
prancing and kicking with undeniable flair.

Demons wail loudly while trekking the clouds,
wind whipping on high and rippling their shrouds.
Long-dead wood fires leave a spectral glow,
thus kindling a beacon for all who would know.

The mers, with their legs, run as fast as they can,
teasing drowned sailors with their light-hearted plan.
But the seamen are rapidly closing the span
and then there will be a great fire to fan.

Such is the sight of the forevermore
just beyond the other side of the door.

SEA WRAITH

The silent night darkens, deep mists roll in.
The heavy damp air bears a palpable skin.
All quiet but light clicking and clapping,
the lapping on the ship, a light tapping.

No birds of kind are there in flight.
No fish of kind are there in sight.
No wind, no breath, no sign of unrest.
All quiet as Nature is wistly depressed.

Slowly, in the mists, a lightening unfolds.
From a distance, a speck grows as it molds.
Something in motion sets over the sea.
Developing, manifesting—not yet to be.

Growing in brightness now, finding a form.
Not so much churning now, the curtain is torn.
Getting much closer now, growing in size.
Developing vague features and definitely eyes.

No more solid than a growing white mist.
No feeling, no action, no volition—all missed.
No substantial existence from what you can see—
only a shimmering of the fog and the sea.

Then clarity is born from the whirling white mists—
a figure, near-human, undoubted exists.
The presence comes gliding, slowly with ease,
her garments all flowing as though in a breeze.

A hooded great cloak flies light in the sway,
holding some features of the figure at bay.
A wispy light gown flows free underneath.
The specter, in whole, as white as your teeth.

Searching for something: a treasure to seize?
One would not know if this would all please.
A grimness of sorts: a daring treatise?
A determined look prompts startled unease.

Beauty well-poised but grace is ill-wrought,
of great misfortune this creature is fraught.
Looking with a glare that was gravely distraught,
finding no comfort from what, we know not.

Long slender hands, bare ankles and feet.
Long thin hair swept around and yet neat.
A face of fine marble—well-chiseled, high-crowned.
Cheeks were high-boned, with eyes almond-round.

No doubt a young lass much loved and bemoaned,
searching all time for a reunion postponed.
One lost at sea she is looking to find
with but her soul and what's left of her mind.

She covered us all with a sweep of her eyes
and then nodded her head in long, painful sighs.
With this last movement, it would not be long.
One moment here, the next moment gone.

May the gods grant her some peace,
for all that is wrong.

FOR LOVE OF THE SEA

The smell of the salt.
The winds that caress my face.
A breath in my ears.
The love of Nature's complexion.

At times aroused,
tempestuous.
At other times quiet,
still, moody.

But mostly fresh,
vibrant, alive.
No wonder man reckons
the sea as a woman.

BUCCANEER ANNE

This lady is loved
by those who sail free—
the greatest of pirates
that ever roamed the sea.

Let there be no doubt—
she takes care of her crew.
But if you're no good,
there's no welcome for you.

Sharks follow her ship
in hopes of a meal.
She feeds them quite well.
They have a splash deal.

If she finds you a lout
with little—no clout,
she'll quick run you through,
turn your insides to out.

If any would argue,
they may well be sent
where Davy Jones tells them
to pay down the rent.

You steal her wheel?
Oh, man! Oh, man!
She'll grab you by the ear.
It'll hurt you so bad,
you'll forever shed a tear.

Her knife she will draw.
Your nose she will peel.
And then she will strap you
to the bottom of her keel.

She doesn't hail port
with a half-empty ship.
You'll come back far richer.
This be a tip!

She's a pleasure to serve
for any swashbuckling gent.
The scourge of the seas,
this lass heaven-sent.

SAILING FREE

In wild leaps we bounded, in wild leaps
we tore a path across the sea.
From crest to crest, we vaulted and swooped
and we soared on our spirit of spree.

Howling through mast-tops and whistling through shrouds—
uncontrolled, in a ruckus of glee—
was the wind of such force, in stable set course,
that our scuppers stayed drenched on the lee.

The sails like white clouds were sweeping across
a sky so deep blue and sun-bright.
Bellied out, as they were, in statuesque form,
they made for a majestic grand sight.

The bow broke the waves into high-flying spray
that soaked the foresails quite through.
These crystalline showers in the sun's shining light
cooled the hearty and hot-blooded crew.

 Awashed with the lee in rushed milky foam
that added to the churning white wake,
the spirited pounding of life's pleasant hours
stretched out in a vacation break.

Thus dancing the seas in joyous delight,
we piped to the chant of a song—
Hey-ho, hey-ho, and what do you know?
—and merrily we bellowed along.

CLOUD SONNET

Yon' clouds in the distance traversing to shore,
once ghosts of small sails just beginning their flight,
 soft-setting the tone for a musical score,
they shimmered and played with the sun and the light.

A forged haze became dainty white fluff,
then a delicate down and white cottony fleece.
Then blanketing the sun, thus playing rough—
grimness now blackening, forecasting no peace.

Tempests of pillars reach high in the sky—
troubled, hastened turmoil—they're cross.
Veils being shed for so much gone awry,
thus dropping their teardrops with staggering loss.

Daughters of Ocean, once clean and white—
now scurried, now hurried, in much dreaded plight.

HEARTY *and* HOT-BLOODED

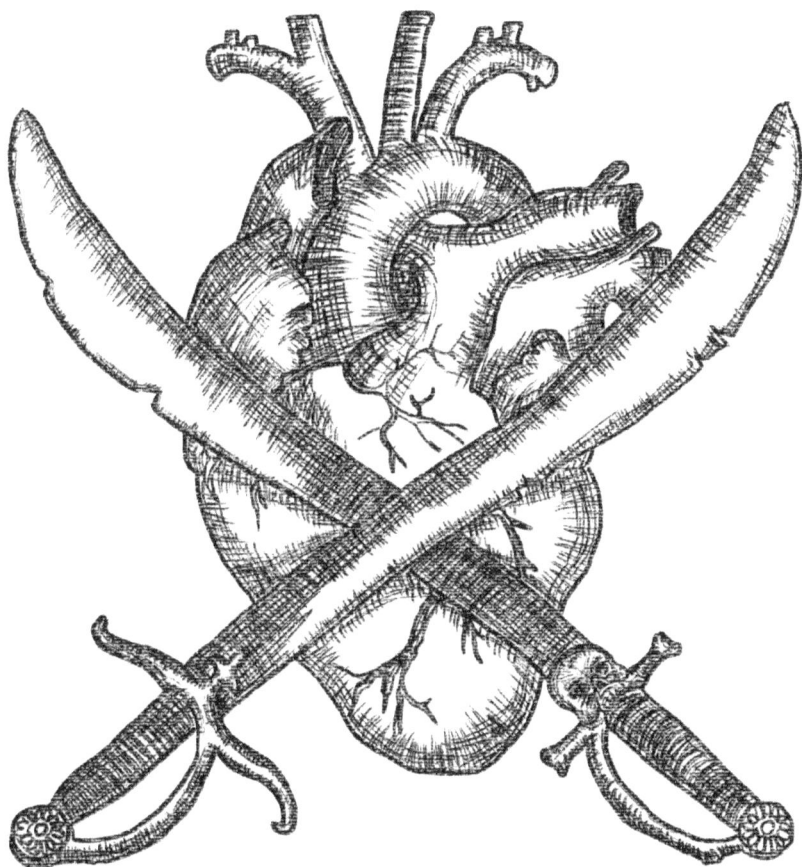

STORM RISING

A coming of storm swells—a roughening sea.
Dark clouds in the distance, in great majesty.
A moment of quiet, a prelude to stress.
Nature's great beauty, winding up in duress.

No longer a breath caressing your ear,
but the shouting of Furies, fear on the shear.
The mounting of tension as the storm comes to pass.
The sailor does penance, thinks of home and his lass.

To rocking calm seas, to rolling with swells.
No haven is near—just tempest that dwells.
The monsters of old stay beyond the tide.
Even they are wanting a safe place to hide.

A wall of green water, the face of the sea
as otherwise formless, no compassion to see.
The demons below in green-water abyss
pay attention to all—no soul there to miss.

The ship settles deep in the trough below,
then climbs steep grades the waves want to throw.
The bow at a slight angle to the swell as it passes,
in hopes that in the upsurge no smashing amasses.

The figurehead swallows the first of the fight.
The bow bounding through, the water holds tight.
A tonnage of water engages the ship.
Under she goes 'til the bow clears the rip.

No man left standing, knocked down with the hit.
The foredeck and castle no longer well-knit.
A quick kick of the wheel, the stern to align
straight up the wave to the top of the brine.

Hoping to heavens the crest's a smooth ride.
The winds pushing hard and curling the tide.
Now down in a hurry to the trough with a crash.
A quick turn of the wheel so the spine will not smash.

So violent the saltwater Furies be.
Men would seek death just for calmness to see.
In a short time now, it's a story to tell
of the unyielding power of unmediated hell.

The watchman does not bother to ring the watch bell.
It strikes on its own—eight bells on the swell.
Demons spout forth with mirth on a wing.
Old Jolly Roger now here,
                              he begins to sing. . . .

NIGHT BOARDING

Dampness and darkness cling to the night air,
fashioning false peace for those who would care.
Wavelets do ripple 'cross the broad beams so fair.
The little fat merchantman better take care.

A gentle low rolling swings the deck and the mast—
cradle of solitude for men looking past.
The lapping of liquid, a sound that is still.
No one has need for a hand on the till.

Lantern be lit for a ship that is still—
the middle of night, a warm beacon in the chill.
The crew all asleep in their hammocks, no drill.
The sentry on duty, two hours to kill.

Mists of the night on a watery sheen.
Men in small boats with eyes that do glean
black silhouettes lining the starry night sky,
cleaving the mists, fooling the eye.

Black the seas upon which they ride.
Shadowy shapes—they flow with the tide.
These little black shapes will form as they will
to little dark boats with a man at the till.

Low to the water in silent-held stealth.
All out to plunder the merchantman's wealth.
The light thump of oars being muffled in felt.
Nothing left loose, all tied with a welt.

Over the bulwarks, the silent men go.
No need for ladders, the scaling is low.
Close to the ramparts with plain and bare feet—
this to ensure their quiet deceit.

Up on the poop deck to check for the watch.
Eight bells won't ring if unaware, he will botch.
Better to wait for the half-hour to ring,
in case anyone's accustomed to hear that bell sing.

Rushing on deck to find hatches below,
seeking the men whose numbers they know.
Hammocks sway lightly to the roll of the seas—
Come on, oh sweet gents. Get up, if you please.

Muskets are pointed at faces that show,
the merchantmen surprised at how little they know.
No muskets are fired, no sword singes the air.
Little disturbed. No, nary a hair.

Captain's fair quarters the pirates do find.
The door swings silent with hinges grease-lined.
Out, dear Captain. We pardon your regret.
Don't get yourself now in a very fine fret.

Over the side the merchantmen go—
straight to the bottom (only Davy would know).
The ship sails toward the clear rising sun,
a new crew aboard having barrels of grim fun.

THE GOOD SHIP, *REVENGE*

In 1717,
the keel was laid.
She carried a whisper—
a dark deal made.

A pirate ship armed,
ten guns on the deck.
A little sloop, surely,
but gunned to the neck.

It lies close to the water,
so fast in light air.
Along with the draught,
a few feet to bear.

Of fore and aft castles,
indeed there be none,
but built up with bulwarks
to protect man and gun.

Two masts on the deck
with a long heavy boom
to carry broad sails,
in light air to bloom.

A wide, broad-backed beam,
thus spacious below
for loot and supplies and
seventy men . . . all to stow.

Thus all is cared for,
most effective for speed.
And plenty of weapons,
should there come a need.

Fast and maneuverable
to track down its prey
and outrun men-o'-war,
should there come a day.

A sleek silhouette
in the setting sun.
A pirate forever,
it answers to none.

The prey to be found
and put under the gun.
The hunting begins—
a mad hit-and-run.

THE DEVIL OF THE DEEP

1.

Ever try to describe a monster
without bothering to do so?
What is left is stammering reaction—
or you're too stunned to say anything . . . at all.

I stand aghast at this sight that I see.
Confounded am I in appalling distain—
stupefied, unnerved, in paralyzed refrain.

So foul this beast in stagnant refuse,
this ulcerous malignancy of Nature unknown,
a plague and a pestilence clear to the bone.

Unwholesome to the fullest, this demon of the deep.
A cankerous affliction, its disease so complete.
So steeped in decay, even devils retreat.

So ill-shaped, misbegotten, this hideous form.
Its horridness beyond all ugliness born,
rancid as it is from feculence torn.

Grim howling to the depths of my being complete.
How deep the soul of man can screech,
beyond the depths of the longest reach.

May the heavens descend to cover the pit—
this abyss so well-known, of notorious fame—
and with it this creature, be rendered the same.

2.

I see the rings on your tentacles quiver,
you stir the depths, a cold-blooded giver.
You hover in silence, drawn to the fray,
preparing to feast on the flesh of your prey.

Dripping green pus down the set of your jaw.
The lines of determination, you're ready to gnaw.
So poisoned your beak, so sharpened to hold,
to restrain for the feast your pleasure unfolds.

Slither and slide over the slime and the dead.
Warm is the meat you'll mangle and shred.
Blood-red, your eyes thus mirror the quest.
The dread feast is coming—
       you will not rest.

HURRICANE

The wind comes to screech,
rage at the dark clouds' despair.
The ocean seethes foul . . .

A calmness resides in the morning's tired light,
for the dawn did not come with the usual bite.
A far bank of gray clouds greets the distant sea-sight
and thus shadows the rays of the sun's blazing might.

A pillow of puffs, faint caress of the cheek.
The breath of the wind so gentle, so meek.
But then, quiet whisper as it wanders through trees
and freshens its voice, as though trying to please.

As morning draws on, there's a darkening frown.
The clouds o'er the sea wear a billowing gown.
No longer the peace of a calm wistful day,
the sun gave the sky one final last ray.

The wind freshens its ardor with bellowing strong voice.
The clouds' troubled turmoil thus picks up the pace.
The wind starts to moan as though fouled with abuse—
an imbalance of Nature's fine-entwined lace.

Clouds once thought distant are hastened, now close,
and in tormented anguish shed tears of despair.
They now rush the land as though caught in a chase—
rolling and rumbling and tossed through the air.

Moans rise in anguish to a wail and a howl—
no more the pause to inhale for breath.
Soon to come shrieking in fiendish tumult,
a screech and a howl with the thrashing of death.

The trees bend with the fear that the storm is so near.
Their submission keeps stride with the wind's angry face.
The loud rustling leaves are blown off the stem.
Limbs are bending in sway, with a frantic wild pace.

The surf pounds the beach with thunderous boom
and thus slams the land loudly on this neighboring shore.
Incoming, it travels 'cross the bight of the land,
a stampede of water rushes to outrun the roar.

SEA FURY

The chronometer falling, the sky whips on past.
Dark seas growing fast and unbound.
Open sea on a ship, rough weather forecast.
In the grip of a gale, here we are found—
buffeted, buffeted, all the way 'round.

Seas roaring up to the shriek of the wind.
Waves come a-rushing, onward they're bound.
Seas to the sky, no use to prescind.
Squalls, planing waves, spindrift unwound—
buffeted, buffeted, all the way 'round.

Bows cutting these seas, plunge deep in the broth.
Rushed water on deck, chaos will confound.
Wavelets to rivulets of foam, bubble, froth.
Raw fatigue and exhaustion, all energy drowned—
buffeted, buffeted, all the way 'round.

Battering squalls of air most profound.
Eardrums imploding with fury of sound.
Screeching wild rage so willing to pound.
Beaten and pummeled and knocked to the ground—
buffeted, buffeted, all the way 'round.

Tormented confusion upon which to dwell.
Wrath of the tempest, delirium well-found.
Death would be better than prolonging this hell.
Mind, body, soul on a merry-go-round—
buffeted, buffeted, all the way 'round.

Hold on.

HONOR IN BATTLE

Plying along calm waters, they came
to march to destiny's beat.
And though it seemed a safe, calm day,
destiny will sometimes cheat.

The two warships took an attentive stand
for sight of an enemy ship.
Then the men at all the mastheads shouted,
Sail, ho! as they tightened their grip.

Finally the class of ships became
so very abundantly clear.
Each spied the other, a square-rigged frigate
of size and appropriate gear.

Still yet, too far a distance to see
the make and flag being flown.
But onto collision a course was set,
spiriting each upon its own.

An excitement wound through both the ships,
as everyone stood abrupt.
The captains yelled with strong command
for action to finally erupt.

*All hands clear the deck for action
and release the guns to bear!*
Both captains thus did ready their ships,
neither of them wanting to err.

Finally, a masthead shout: *No doubt!*
The colors clearly show—
the flags of the approaching frigate ships
designated them as foe.

All men attend to their duty now,
the battle cry did sound.
Every man thus scrambled for his post,
all battle stations found.

The guns were shotted, the matches lit,
the arms were passed around.
All stood still in quiet suspense,
as the ships were forward bound.

Finally close enough for cannon range,
the crews did let them loose.
The silence broken o'er the calm blue seas—
no quarter given, no truce.

The boom of cannon, the crack of ball
striking both the ships.
A tremendous roar, a thunderous dirge,
a senseless feeling rips.

The sails were shred, the masts took lead,
the pieces falling 'round.
Splinters flying and men dying
and still the cannons did pound.

And more than half the companies' men
lay dead or dreadfully downed.
And body parts lay here and there.
And still the cannons did pound.

The smaller frigate, now out of ball,
used every small thing in sight.
Bits of wood and chain, 'til nothing remained,
nothing but the coming night.

The men all fighting bravely with
the mind's eye kept in check,
for destruction lay upon everything
and blood ran down the deck.

Yells and screams were loudly heard
amongst the cannon din.
The pain and suffering of wounded men
succumbed to their will to win.

Yet for all the destruction taking place
and the heavy human tolls,
the men still fighting kept a cheer
to distract their horrified souls.

Fighting brave and cheerfully
was the best that could be done.
For any other option—naught—
for in fact there was but one.

No time for reaction or reflected thought
or remorse of any kind,
only time to fight the fear and shout
the battle cry to bind.

The smaller ship went abruptly quiet
as cannon fire did quit,
with nothing left to fire across
but shredded rags and spit.

No sails worth banding, no mast left standing,
no motion nor way to go.
The captain of the smaller ship saw
defeat in the endless row.

Rise up and strike the bunting, said he,
and with sorrow the crew complied.
They knew the battle was lost and done,
thus all the clamor died.

The silence fell with sudden shock
as the surrender flag was set.
All stood in the stark mute of confusion,
the senses and mind upset.

Both captains met on the small frigate deck
to negotiate the term.
Being noble-bearing gentlemen,
they held their stature firm.

The defeated captain did offer his sword
in fine ceremonious respect.
Though shame he felt at the loss of his ship,
with the Fates he could not object.

Of matters now the victor spoke
concerning the present plight.
Both ships had taken such heavy tolls
from the long and bitter fight.

You have been honorably defeated
in this battle bravely fought.
I fear no reprisal on your part, for it is
as gentlemen, we are taught.

Please take your sword and retain it for,
to say with some subtlety,
it is a dishonor you do me otherwise
and I desire your company.

It was a battle bravely fought,
although outmanned, outgunned.
And you lost the steering of this fine ship,
for the winds the Fates not dunned.

You took good care of your ship and men—
for this I salute you too.
Your command would not fault to commend
the acts of one as brave as you.

For now, let us bury those, our men,
who have fallen, but in good grace.
For whether a battle is won or lost,
our comrades we embrace.

And so the two fine captains banded
and together did the rites.
For all the men who had perished there,
there were no further fights.

The dead were sewn up in their hammocks—
the familiar cloth they bound.
Their messmates then did carry their bundles
on gratings, straight and sound.

And down the row of seamen all
to the leeward bow, port side.
The messmates carried their brethren sweet.
Both crews, now one, all cried.

And after all the battles wrought
and disputes of every kind,
there is one fact that binds us all:
We are brothers—all mankind.

In honor, bravery, and duty bound,
a deep respect is ground.
It matters little which foe is more sound,
if wickedness is not profound.

We commit our brothers to the deep,
the chaplain loud did cry.
And each sailor bore a saddened face
and passed a woeful sigh.

The bodies fell to the waters deep
as the gratings were lifted high.
And all were found deep in thought
at all that had passed them by.

BLACKBEARD'S END

The Governor of Virginia, having received
such numerous bitter complaint,
issued by proclamation a sound reward,
to remove the pirate taint.

Edward Teach, Blackbeard by fame,
had crossed too many a line.
And in pardons bought and in lies well-caught,
he finally did hamper his design.

The Governor hired two shallow-draft sloops
for a lieutenant well-qualified,
and a complement of sixty men
and a midshipman by the name of Hyde.

Small arms and swords and pistols in all
were the lot that they could carry.
The sloops were small, to clear the shoals,
so cannons they could not ferry.

Off they set to find their prey,
following rumors at best.
Of Blackbeard's ship the stories abounded
as to where the *Adventure* did rest.

At dusk upon that fateful eve,
through many days of search,
the *Adventure* was found at Ocracoke,
anchor dropped at her perch.

The lieutenant chose to wait for the morn
to check the tide and shoal.
And so he rested a peaceful night—
the fight would be taking its toll.

Blackbeard and crew did party 'til late,
though aware the unknown ships.
A drinking bout, they had their fun,
while entertaining friends with their quips.

The lieutenant commanded one of the sloops
and Hyde had command of the other.
Their thought was to rush the *Adventure* at dawn,
while the pirates were still in a dither.

The *Adventure*—nine cannons lying still in their mounts.
The pirates still did not care.
If only the sloops could come alongside
before they were brought to bear.

To board the *Adventure* before they were hit
was the lieutenant's well-thought-out plan.
But Hyde's sloop and then the lieutenant's
hit the shoals in a very short span.

As grounded they were, the surprise was now gone
and the crew of the *Adventure* took note.
Running toward them, their purpose was clear
and Blackbeard took charge of his boat.

As the ballast was thrown to get off of the shoal,
so the sloops could move on and attack,
Blackbeard and crew sprang to action—be damned—
no time to sit in the sack.

In these critical moments, establishing grounds,
near-panic was set at a high.
The sloops were desperate to free themselves
and Blackbeard set pace—*do or die.*

The pirates acted to loosen their sails
and cut loose their anchor from the ground.
Their cannons were manned and stations were set.
They readied to throw a fast round.

The wind was slight, the sails billowed light,
so the sloops were powered by oar.
Their hulls finally lightened, the crews now less frightened,
on the move they were once more.

Now close enough that the muskets could fire,
both started burning their powder.
Blackbeard, ranging on one of the sloops,
let blast the four- and six-pounder.

Hyde's sloop took the brunt of the pirates' first blast
and Hyde was killed with a shot.
The deck was ravaged, the foresails were downed,
and the sloop was stopped on the spot.

The oarsmen were mangled and blood swept the deck,
but some action took place so profound.
A few men returned musket arms-fire
and sometimes luck did astound.

A ball clipped the halyard of the fleeing ship.
All the foresails collapsed like a tent.
The ship thus slowed, it could not make escape,
for the oarsmen were rowing hell-spent.

Blackbeard did hail them as closure was sure,
he wanted to know: *Why harass?*
And he cursed and damned them, belittled by name,
as he drank the liquor in his glass.

The lieutenant had failed to carry his ploy
and time had signaled the end.
For as fast as the oarsmen continued to row,
their grounding they could not transcend.

Blackbeard then decided it was fight to the end—
no quarter to give or to take.
He was sure of himself; his cannons were ready;
the lieutenant's sloop he did rake.

The cannons were shotted with partridge and grape
to make an end of the day.
Grenades that they made of rum bottles and iron
were thrown on the sloop in the fray.

Many men on the sloop were slashed into bits—
twenty would not fight there again.
But obscured in the smoke, the lieutenant did hide
the last of his non-injured men.

What was left of his men, down the hatch to the hold,
the ladder they did quickly descend.
And Blackbeard thought that they were done.
There seemed no one left to contend.

And so Blackbeard boarded in front of his crew
to tie off the fine sloop, now sought.
With so few men left standing, the ship was his
to add to his pilfered lot.

Up pushed the lieutenant with men on the run
to stop the fooled boarding, small band.
And leading their crews, the two leaders faced off,
each with a sword in his hand.

The fighting was fierce, in a few minutes done,
both sides taking a worthy stand.
But the weary seamen, what left of the crew,
slaughtered the small boarding band.

Blackbeard was killed with five musket-borne shots
and twenty large grievous cuts.
By then, Hyde's old sloop did come alongside
with their muskets' fast-sounding rebuts.

What was left of the crews made a brave final stand,
allowing victory to take shape.
Some pirates did fight, while some tried to run,
but none were allowed to escape.

The *Adventure* was theirs, the reward in large share,
and so was the sailors' delight.
On *Adventure*'s bowsprit, the trophy was hung—
Blackbeard's head in cursed plain sight.

Legend would leave us a peculiar strong note,
as Blackbeard was thrown to the sea.
Headless he swam 'round the *Adventure* three times.
The curse was not finished, you see.

And a printer's apprentice who was looking for pay,
Ben Franklin had said as he wrote of the day,
in a fine published piece that ended this way—

It's better to swim in the sea below
than to swing in the air and feed the crow,
says jolly Ned Teach of Bristol.

MAN OVERBOARD

a villanelle

I grieve and do penance, my soul not to rot,
but spirits have spoken—all shipmates despair.
But death is not evil, if hereafter is not.

My shipmate, my friend, oh my brethren begot,
did fall o'er the side, his condition a scare.
I grieve and do penance, my soul not to rot.

Few seamen can swim well to save their own lot.
Few crewmen would rescue—hell may well care.
But death is not evil, if hereafter is not.

The gods of the seas require tribute, we are taught—
a debt to be paid, a blood offering to spare.
I grieve and do penance, my soul not to rot.

An offering of sorts is what ought to be wrought.
To meddle with spirits, it's best you not err.
But death is not evil, if hereafter is not.

So I and the crew stood still as we ought,
and did what best—let the gods take what's fair.
I grieve and do penance, my soul not to rot.
But death is not evil, if hereafter is not.

ACROSS *this* DEAD GLASS SEA

TYPHOON

An elegant sunrise awoke the chill morning dew,
warming the air as the darkness was won.
But the distant sky warned of change yet to come.
It blazed with red-golds while hailing the sun
      and thus the light's rays like blown glass were spun.

As morning progressed, it was abundantly clear
that there was a far bank of thick clouds to fear.
A sobering stiff wind, its buffets sincere,
with fitful strong intention, this wind begged to rear—
      a rapid unraveling of a dark atmosphere.

Once then a sea of restful calming breath,
of rolled gentle swell and azure appeal,
now a confusion of waves and restless slop.
A sea of gray pewter now kicking its heel,
      misfortune's element when freshened with zeal.

Far from safe waters and a hospitable port,
brave men and brave ships will dance to this jig.
All tied down and secured and lashed to the deck,
the snapping of canvas and the rattle of rig—
      ship-speak for the coming; no chance to renege.

Billowing sails stretch alive with the sway,
excitement at first as the ship's running free.
Of constant felt purpose are the wind and sea,
everything rushing with strong gaiety—
      a taste of wildness as the wind blows to lee.

Surfing the seas, slightly shuddered and thrown,
with a freshening voice the wind starts to moan.
Thus calling the clouds to seek their new home,
the ship's stays begin singing refrains of their own.
       What is coming will certainly darken the tone. . . .

The wind is now whining and wailing with might.
The clouds have now thickened to cover the blight.
The waves with dark majesty stand more upright.
The squalls throw the rain to add to the spite.
       Nature comes howling to strike man from its sight.

The wind shears the wave-tops to smothering spume.
The hissing of froth and driven rain through the air
adds to the chaos to which none can compare,
and stinging like needles to add to the fare,
       breathing comes in constant withering despair.

The stretch of the sails and the tug on the sheets
cause the seamen to furl them, if they're to keep.
The ship now trembling and quivering and pitching headlong,
as it falls to the trenches and plows waves too steep.
       The wind blowing angry—destruction to reap.

Walls of water on deck as waves roll on past.
Swirls of foam gush up to meet the stinging spray.
The side of the lee buried deep in the sea.
No more division between the sky and the fray—
       submerged, from the heavens to where devils will play.

But then comes the final shriek-driven pitch—
the screech, the roar, of a fiendish tumult.
The ship staggers up walls to plunge to the abyss.
This rouses the waves, which the wind will exalt.
       The rage of the tempest thus assaults the occult.

A last smothered thought—how unearthly the scream.
To the power of Nature, all is resigned.
As the mind and the body meld with the storm,
the senses no longer are owned by the mind.
       Driven is the elemental to tie and to bind.

Though with words we give it emotion and push,
the truth is that, beyond the scale of the threat,
there is no emotion, no malice of thought,
but only the sighs of Nature's balance unmet.
       For whatever the outcome, there is no regret.

DEATH OF THE *REVENGE*

Captain Bonnet holed up
on a river—Cape Fear.
The good ship, *Revenge*,
much repair in arrears.

Spars were sent down,
most gear went ashore.
Long lines from masts
to the trees there and more.

Timber replaced,
the old broken free.
Thus the mighty hull was slick,
slippery as the sea.

Barnacles hacked off,
down to bare wood and seam.
Worms dug, holes patched,
the tar smooth like cream.

Ship brand-spanking-new,
the crew paid the toll.
So Colonel Rhett thought
from the side of the shoal.

The Colonel did wait
for Bonnet to out.
In the mouth of the river,
two war sloops to rout.

Bonnet well-knew
it was fight best or be done.
Little luck or not,
this gun versus gun.

Gun carriages greased,
the barrels were clean.
Bright shiny cannons
would sing out on the scene.

Heavy cloth wrappings,
for the bulwarks were took,
to stop flying splinters—
so says the book.

Light sails were stowed
for a canvas with coat.
'Lum a retardant,
a fire not to tote.

Rigging was doubled,
standing by chain.
If sails go a-flying,
there's nothing to gain.

Blankets were piled,
oakum plugs set,
just to make sure,
but not ready yet.

Stations for battle,
grenades to prepare.
Stinkpots of sulfur
smelled up the light air.

Culverin blunderbuss
ready to go
and each man armed
from his head to his toe.

One cutlass apiece,
plus five pistols to boot.
A large band of belts
to hold it all mute.

Up anchor! he called.
Dawn brought a light breeze.
Down the river to go
through a tight squeeze.

Sponges wet,
matches lit,
gunports open,
the smart cannons sit.

Two war sloops waited
just 'round the bend—
the *Revenge* their target,
a hard mark to rend.

The little sloop fast—
light-footed, sleek, sound—
skirted the war sloops,
but went fast aground.

Too close to the bank,
so close to the sea.
Yet as luck would have it,
so stuck were the three.

But *Revenge* was thus last
to recover from ground.
And by then she had taken
quite a few round.

With great pomp and correctness,
Bonnet said: *Nay!*
He surrendered the *Revenge*,
a white flag that day.

All men were hanged,
found guilty the same.
For a pirate—no deal.
He goes back where he came.

The fate of the ship,
no one knows—what a shame.
But wherever it ended,
no more the same.

SHIPWRECK

Down on the beach, a peaceful scene—
all calm and quiet and very serene.
Small waves lapping, quietly slapping the shore.
A relaxing of Nature from the tenseness before.

Hurricanes blow through the isles by the score,
twisting and turning 'round a strong-centered core.
With towering tempest and deafening roar,
through the isles these maelstroms blasted and tore.

One storm's sacrifice lies out on the reef—
a warship well-battered beyond all relief.
The scars from its battles lead one to believe
it was abandoned and given a last parting leave.

Left to float or sink, as the gods would please,
long drifting on tides and shoved by the seas.
Near-finished before the storms took the helm,
hurricane season could well overwhelm.

Overcome as it was by the blasting great flow,
as the gale whipped froth the fierce waves would throw,
then came torrents of rain in bludgeoning blows
and walls of great water that knocked it below.

It was not buried, but cast on its grave.
The winds and the waves left little to save.
Tossed by the seas as rejected and scorned—
of foreign nature and not to be mourned.

Ran hard on the reef, a large coral thorn—
back to the land from whence it was born.
A blast, a knock, a shock by all means—
timbers to splinters, smashed smithereens.

Impaled on the reef, it has a slight list.
At times it looks floating on a low-skimming mist.
But float it never will, the hull is well-shot
and encrusted by barnacle, plundered by rot.

Topmasts hang broken, tangled in shroud,
in utter destruction, as all have avowed.
The yardarms are askew to which tattered sails cling.
The sails torn to rag strips and shredded long string.

Blocks, sheets, and stays are in tangled array,
in webs of despair and drooping dismay.
What's left of the sails is weeping the mist,
all feeding the rot—a ship-sized black cyst.

Lodestone in the binnacle, wavering slight.
A slow rock to the deck as though nursing the blight.
The black wheel swings lightly to take up the slack.
The rudder won't move—jammed in its track.

The cavern, its bottom, the holes in its sides,
leave plenty of windows for evening's high tides.
The picture slow-changes with the rolling wave crests,
for in the troughs to follow, the swells find new quests.

As it decays and succumbs to Nature's strong force,
a thought is forthcoming in touching remorse.
Though originally a creation of Man's strong fit hand,
it is Nature, yet, that still has command.

FATHOMS DEEP

From the stout frothy crests to heaven
to the troughs, they bounded and tore.
And there from the pit, they undug themselves,
then up again once more.

The spectacle was sorely grand.
The noble ship was born
like a weed ripped out and tossed aside
at the mercy of the seas' untamed scorn.

The seas in such wild raging commotion.
From billow to billow, they soared.
As the tempest roared in feral-wrought fury,
they were beaten to "smitheres" deeply scored.

Waves that were lashed by the seething tempest
were turned to a sparkling white foam.
And they hissed and thrashed and whistled on past
and drove the vengeance home.

No voice could warn them of the danger.
No hand outstretched to save.
No choice was there, no hope to bear,
and all to a watery grave.

PIRATE KIN

Two warring chiefs, a tribal grudge,
a score to settle sore.
These neighboring clans of seafaring folk
all had been to war.

And now that fragile peace was made
with English and Scottish lords,
the clans of all the Irish coast
had taken up their swords.

The galleys they manned to settle disputes
had one sail and many an oar.
And swiftly they fell to battle it out,
to end it all at grief's door.

These ships they sailed had swivel guns
placed between the oars
and matchlock muskets and arrows and darts—
enough to square up their scores.

One caught head-on, the decks were raked.
From bow to stern, they tore.
This one then swung dead-fast abeam
and their guns let loose a roar.

Many holes appeared in sail and gear;
and shrouds and blocks did fall.
And masts were splintered and men were shredded,
so effective was small shot and ball.

A child did stow on board one ship,
deep within the hold.
The son of the captain, one warring chief—
only six years, all told.

A Gaelic son, a leader born,
with kindness at his command.
With flaming red hair and freckled face,
well he bore the brand.

The boy was famed throughout the land
for his courage of friendliness.
But a little warrior brave and true,
his father would say, no less.

By his own, a child of charitable goodwill
with upright honesty long sown.
To all near clans, friend and foe alike,
his spotless innocence well-known.

The child did finally run up from the hold,
his concern for his father borne strong.
Not only this, but the screams and the pounding
foretold that something was wrong.

On the deck he did scramble, so blindly aghast,
all taken in, in a flash.
He stood in a stupor. The crew tried to shield him,
as the galleys were going to clash.

A broadside was borne, both sides let roar,
and the child's head was fatally smashed.
He fell to the deck in a pool of red blood
and to him his father thus dashed.

The father and crew stood frozen dead-still
at a sight that they could not abide.
A tiny frail boy of innocence well-loved,
a wooden sword and shield by his side.

The captain-father closed his eyes
and his hair he did rend.
And he opened his mouth as if to wail.
But for his mind, nothing would mend.

Silence did settle upon the deck
and the colorful clan flag was struck.
The white flag was hoisted in silent distain.
In total distress, they were stuck.

The father did lift the child of his blood
above his head straight-armed
to show the captain of the enemy ship
the child had thus been harmed.

The captain of the rival ship did see
what irreparable harm had come.
He would rather have burned in hell
than shoulder a grief grown numb.

Loud he howled in rage and grief
for a boy who would make all proud.
The wound was far too deep to bear—
the gods should not have allowed.

He ceased the action and struck his colors
and raised them upside down—
a sickened ship in great distress,
a dirge in funeral gown.

The crews did stand and the ships did part
with a bitter, strangled weep.
They never were to engage again.
Their hearts were burdened deep.

For a child is led by innocent ways—
no sin, no guilt, no—none.
The maker of life from heaven above
now holds dear the little one.

It is later for Man to find foolish ways
and bake on hellfire's rhumb,
the soul to shriek in endless plight
for what they may become.

SEA WITCH

A night as dark as the devil's keep.
The stars won't show, the mists run deep.
Damp and heavy, cold and dense.
But nothing to foretell what would happen hence.

On the masthead, a flashing glow,
though not uncommon at night.
But this was not the usual glow—
the color a ghastly white.

St. Elmo's fire as usually seen
is blue in color, hissing mean.
But never was it a sinister sight—
no spirit-candles were seen.

An ooze of bright effluence
dripped down to the deck.
A crackling, popping, hissing,
with breathing down the neck.

The crew did wonder at this encounter.
That this was mischief, there was no doubter,
for nothing about it boded so well.
The devil's own work it might foretell.

Then spawned from the light,
a dark shadow was rent—
a vaporous cast,
a catastrophic portent.

Dark hair and dark skin
from what they could see.
But then the white highlights
brought substance to be.

A featureless dress
covered by a cloak,
deep-hooded and long,
could be seen in the smoke.

Eye sockets deep,
foreboding, and dark—
large pools thus hollowed
for dread eyes, so stark.

Eyes flashing wildness
with malevolent intent.
Snarling teeth bared—
carnivorous the scent.

High stern cheeks.
Strong cavernous jaw.
Hungry for feast,
voracious the maw.

Filling all voids,
everywhere she seemed.
Jealous mad rage,
joyous, she screamed.

She hovered about
for fresh victims to find.
The heavy air billowed,
as she glided behind.

Her shadow would vary
to fill up the space,
and with it her strength,
with which she'd debase.

We'd heard of this witch, this afflicted malaise.
Its unwholesomeness wanton, a fire in her gaze.
Of jealous intent, there was little to doubt.
Of human virtue, she was wanting to rout.

Once quite human and considerably fair,
the gods did rejoice in her presence, with care.
But vanity overwhelmed, her arrogance amassed.
Then the gods realized her mischief surpassed.

For all of her beauty, no virtue was found.
They told her she was hideously unsound.
She'd tricked and deceived them for favors to spare.
And now that they knew her, they sought to impair.

She was cast to the underworld to burn like a flare.
But with her powers, she would not stay there.
Occasionally, she managed to find her way out,
then revenged on the humans—their virtues stamped out.

From the fires of hell, henceforth she came
to the seas of the Earth to put out the flame.
The land and the heat she avoided with care.
Singed and in pain, she would not dare.

No thoughts of redemption or changing her way,
only thoughts of destruction could hold her at bay.
No cage could confine her that she couldn't traverse.
Her victims—she'd find them with a scourge and a curse.

Humans she blamed deep down in her core.
Her insanity—thinking she'd change what she wore
and bathe in the blood, the flowing red gore.
The gods would have humans to dote on no more.

With the gaze of a demon,
she would freeze her catch.
For mortal humans,
there is no match.

Her shriek of great rapture,
the nourishment of terror.
Unsatiated revenge—
its starvation, an error.

No real attention.
No cause to reflect.
No thought for kind mercy.
It's time to collect.

The ship stood dark
in a cloud of emotion
strung high as the fires—
ecstasy's devotion.

The men on the deck
she snatched with such ease.
No thought to run,
they dropped to their knees.

Their brains did not freeze them
in shock at her sight,
for they were already
petrified by the light.

Their eyes glazed over
without a sound.
The screech of the witch
was well-nigh profound.

The fast-beating heart,
the target to tear.
The bench of all virtue,
too much to bear.

With quick-flying thrust,
her greed-driven hand
dug under the ribcage
with efficient command.

Blood-thirsty long fingers
with ravenous nails
cut through the tissue
to the heart she assails.

The warm heart she clasped,
its beating like thunder.
It palpitated in fear
as she pulled it from under.

Accentuated pops,
arteries asunder.
Well-stretched beyond
any rigid wonder.

Blood showered the deck
as the heart was ripped out.
She ate it still beating,
her craving devout.

Where once there were forty, now there is but one.
Of fine-standing men, just one left undone.
The boiling vile feculence, depravity still here,
and probably will be 'til dawn's light is near.

My journal I leave here for all who would see.
The only one left on this cursed ship is me.
By the grace of the gods, I'm still of sound mind—
a long-journeyed sailor, the last of my kind.

GHOST SHIP

Deep is the night though lit by full moon.
Closed in like a blanket, the doldrums did swoon.
Wisps of low fog drift over the face—
the moon paints the sea in silvery lace.

Stillness as silent as the ocean can reap.
For untold centuries, the secrets to keep.
The mists dampen all sound to a whispered muffle.
The small wavelets subdued, the laps just a snuffle.

Across the dying moon, across this dead glass sea,
hails a ghostly ship—a specter gliding free.
So yellow this moon dipping into the sea,
silhouetting this ship, as black as can be.

No living hand on board to show it a way.
No life to be found to hold it in sway.
Adrift it is, with no direction or scheme.
Deserted by all, or so it would seem.

No sound did it make, but a creak and low groan.
No emotion nor thought was unearthed in the tone.
No breath did escape past the hush of the night.
Thus holding its peace, in its weariness, outright.

Mournful, despairing, its long journey past.
Gone are the glories of battles amassed.
Abandoned, forgotten by its maker's strong hand.
Left to the tides with none to command.

Long looking in silence for the port of its dreams.
No hand on the tiller, lost as it seems.
No hand to guide to a last resting place.
No maker but human to bring long-lasting grace.

LIGHTHOUSE

flash

Dark cold
windswept
are the waves
and the night.

Flash

A tall
silhouette,
distant posture
just right.

FLASH

Perhaps
the last
monument
of mankind
alight.

FL-ASH

Or maybe
a hot fire
and a warm
meal tonight.

FL-ASH!

FELLOWSHIP

I feel the Almighty's breath on me
as the wind upon my bone.
And though I may be by myself,
I know I'm not alone.

I take a deep and quenching breath
of the essence of this life
and fill my lungs with the Spirit's blessing,
in a corporeal world so rife.

I walk along this patch of sand
and scuff along a trail
and meander here, now back and forth.
This course may tell a tale.

The light crunch I hear as I walk along
this soft and pliable sand,
it is the voice of a thousand grains
all under Nature's command.

With my hand, I scoop a bit of earth
and through my fingers find,
from ashes to ashes and dust to dust,
I have discovered like kind.

As though it were
WRITTEN IN SAND

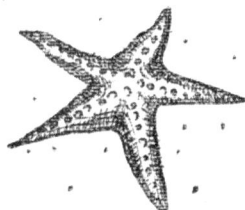

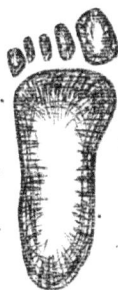

A SEA OF SOLITUDE

One day I came upon the sea
and the restfulness came as a place for me.
So warm, so wet. The sounds that rolled,
as in the womb, I felt the hold.

So tired in body, so tired in mind.
Back to elemental rhythms undefined—
the clack of crab, the cry of gull,
the water washing a ship's wooden hull.

Oh, to drift with the tides and roll with the sea
and blow with the wind, gently pushed to the lee.
I give myself up to the touch and the smell,
the sound of it all—clear sight bodes well.

Time is not measured; the eternal is sown.
The beach is swept clean, clear to the bone.
Here is the emptiness of being alone,
of bare open measure, freedom the throne.

Ultimate harmony here to seek—
no conflict, no choices, no emotional peak.
All thoughts are thus drowned in solitude's grace.
The waves wash the sand of humanity's trace.

A clarity found in this infinite space—
a rebirth, a baptism, which won't erase.
Reawakening thought, inspiration is gleaned.
Where perplexity existed, the lens now is cleaned.

BEACH SOUNDS, PART 1

The Voice

Cccaaa-ur
An indescribable sound of a million voices
resounding in a deep-roared barrage
of clashing opinion and crashing emotion,
smacking into the beach with breaking undertones,
blending into harmonious discord of ambiguity
meaning nothing, but soothing nonetheless.

Sshh-ish
Bubbles popping, froth slopping, sand pebbles get their mopping.
A random dissipation, all voices to quell.
Relaxing the motion, suspending the commotion
with a short and swift rush.

Sshh-ush
Asking for a hush,
a repose of quiet for a calm breath,
a moment of reflection, for yet more attention,
as the cycle repeats in endless progression.

NATURE'S CALL

The seagulls are flying
to grab beakfuls, if they dare—
should they land on a picnic
with a few bites to spare.

The curlews are stalking
and chased by the comb.
They hunt crabs in the sand
and dig down through the loam.

The pelicans are swimming
with the roll of the wave.
They're looking down under,
scooping up what they crave.

Such is the morning,
an early enough sight.
All birds are feeding
with ample delight.

SEA'S HEALING

a Petrarchan sonnet

Let my soul be calmed by gentle ocean spray,
for a path of meaning beyond this life's confusion.
Let the waves sway clearness of mind to soften delusion.
The tide will ebb and flow despite man's decay.

As tracks disturb the sand along the bay,
our troubles trample heavily upon emotion.
Our burdens break the strings of a calming notion,
but the sea with tranquil sounds does wash them away.

For Nature's alcoves awaken a calming respect.
Although the troubles that challenge our life entail
a great and necessary part on which we reflect,

we look with hope to see beyond the gale,
out near and far for something not clearly wrecked,
to stake firm ground and discern a steadfast trail.

BEACH SOUNDS, PART 2

The Orchestration

A thousand hands clapping in rising acclaim.
A wave building far off, let loose from the tame.
A pounding-down beat, the thunder well-felt.
The waves pound the beach, the sand takes the belt.

A rising staccato, beginning to melt.
A sand pebble chorus sings the pelting they're dealt.
The accented pops of bubbling froth
make delicate the ripple at the end of the swath.

Quiet pools are emptied and filled by design.
Coral pockets are found still holding their brine.
Clumps of seaweed add to the iodine smell.
The salty sea air is encrusted as well.

Even here by the sea, many small creatures dwell,
for life is robust, as the ages do tell.
Anemones and starfish are easy to find
and other small creatures of similar kind.

Rivulets—some gushing, some dripping, confined—
rushing back down, age-old outlets are lined.
The waves rolling back with some magical beat—
 vague syncopation to the chorus, complete.

OCEAN SUNRISE

A gray dawn before the morning light.
An orange flare to break the sleepy night.
A few clouds hanging there in distant sight.
Upon the water, a mist holds tight.

The squawk of seabirds calling to the day.
The giant frigates having the most to say.
The seals and dolphins beginning their play—
just waking up and making their way.

A heavy blanket of hazy air solidified.
The sea, gray and blue-green, pulled by the tide.
Faraway wavelets now glance and dance.
The light permeates the now tender trance.

The damp salt air, the breath of the sea
upon inhaling, awakens and sets free.
The coldness of dew warmed by first light
revives the sailor's good morning delight.

SHIPPING OUT

There's a schooner bright and pretty
with a crew list yet to be.
And I'm well-set for a wandering along
the highways of the sea.

And when I'm ready for leaving behind
these chaotic bights of land,
I'll have no regrets nor sorrow nor grief
as the ship slips past the strand.

So far away, another land
to which the ship must go.
But where and when I do not care
but to be in Nature's flow.

The wind, the waves, the ocean ways—
for these I'll take a stand.
For human workings, I have no praise,
but the sea's intricacies I understand.

FREEDOM

Let my soul be as free as the sea.
Let the waves as they roll, roll over me.
—This forever and as long as can be.

Let the winds of my soul touch my heart,
so that thoughts of pure form have a start
and render gentle words to impart.

And the words shall set conscious direction
giving rise to my aware circumspection
and identifying my deep introspection.

And so through the mists would I see
to a new and refined degree—
my gaze on the world to roam free.

For the sea knows well of taciturnity,
of the language of silently sought tranquility,
and the deepness of poetic thought in clarity.

The comfort of knowing Life's hand,
as though it were written in sand,
is the pathway I will understand.

And the song of the Spirit's call
lying beneath the sea-surface squall
will stir my beating heart to enthrall.

Deep as the sea lies my sanity.
Understanding, a compelled amenity,
as the sea rolls on for eternity.

ENDNOTES

1. **"Sea Song"** was first published in *Ocean Magazine*, summer 2012.

2. **"Sailing Free"** was inspired by the work, "She Was Alive, Immortal!" in the book *Tarpaulin Muster*, by John Masefield.

3. **"The Good Ship, *Revenge*"** was inspired by the historical narrative, "Pirate Ship: The Revenge," in the book *Tall Ships and Great Captains*, by A.B.C. Whipple.

4. **"Hurricane"** was first published in *WestWard Quarterly*, spring 2012.

5. **"Honor in Battle"** was inspired by the narrative provided by Samuel Leech, the fifth gunner on the British thirty-eight-gun man--of-war *H.M.S. Macedonian* as it engaged the forty-four-gun *U.S.S. United States* in 1812.

6. **"Blackbeard's End"** was inspired by the historical narrative, *The Republic of Pirates*, by Colin Woodard, 2007, pages 289–297.

7. **"Death of the *Revenge*"** was inspired by the historical narrative, "Pirate Ship: The Revenge," in the book *Tall Ships and Great Captains*, by A.B.C. Whipple.

8. **"Fathoms Deep"** was inspired by "The Red Flag at the Fore" in the book *Sea Stories by an Old Sailor*, author unknown.

ABOUT THE AUTHOR

Joseph L. Bensinger is the author of four poetry collections: *Man, Ships, and the Sea*; *Of Curses and Blessings*; *Journeys through the Tapestry*; and *Beginnings and Ends*. His poems have appeared in *Haiku Journal*, *WestWard Quarterly*, *Ocean Magazine*, and *Mobius*. Before retiring, he worked as an electronics project engineer, a computer systems manager, and a teaching anthropologist. He now spends his time writing ethnohistory and poetry. Bensinger lives with his family in Washington.